Frogs, frogs, FROGS.

You can find frogs almost
everywhere there is water.
They live in ponds and in
the woods. Some even
live in sewers under
a city street.

EASY in the Water

Frogs have amazing skin. It is smooth and moist. It lets in water so a frog can spend a long time in ponds or other bodies of fresh water. It never needs to drink because it gets all the water it needs through its skin.

GREEN FROG

Splash!

This frog pushes through water with long, strong legs and webbing on its feet.

A frog is WATCHING!

A frog can float for hours with

only its eyes above the waterline.

That's because it can breathe through

its skin. It takes in oxygen dissolved in

water and expels carbon dioxide.

A Frog JUMPS

Because almost all frogs have lungs, they are just as much at home on land as in the water.

Most frogs are jumpers.

The legs that help them swim can also send them soaring into the air to chase prey or to escape an enemy.

RED-EYED TREE FROG

A frog's long, strong hind legs stretch out all the way in mid-jump.

Frog have extra-flexible shoulders and hip bones to take the shock of all that JUMPING!

The SEE-THRU Frog

Frogs look different from us on the outside,

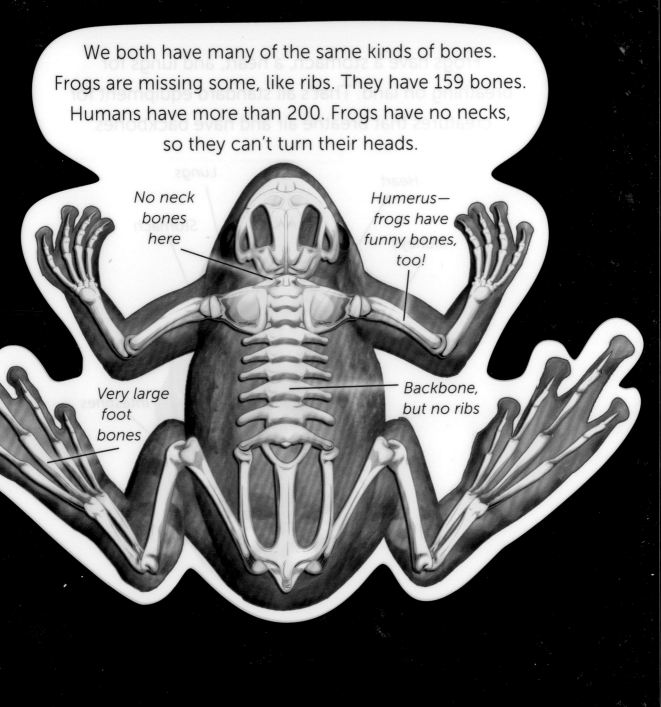

Frogs have a stomach, a heart, and lungs for breathing on land. That's all standard equipment for creatures that breathe air and have backbones.

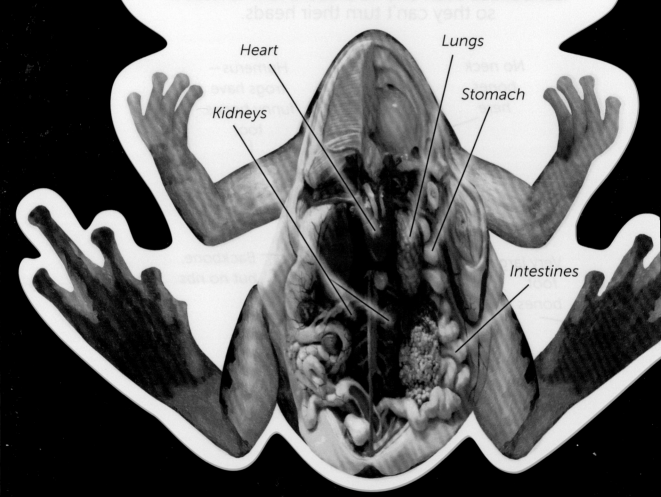

Heart

Lungs

Stomach

Kidneys

Intestines

This view shows the belly—or the ventral side—
of a frog. It is always lighter in color than the
back—or dorsal—side.

but on the inside we are pretty similar.

A FROG or a TOAD?

AMERICAN TOAD

A toad is a kind of frog.

It often has drier, bumpier skin and spends more time on land than a frog. It also has shorter legs. That makes it easier to catch than a frog, but it is more likely to bite.

GREEN MARSH FROG

This **spadefoot** is froglike and toadlike.

It has vertical (up-and-down) pupils like many frogs but bumpy skin like many toads.

COMMON SPADEFOOT

Toads have bumpy skin.

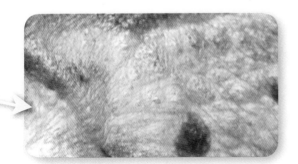

Frogs have smooth skin.

vertical pupil

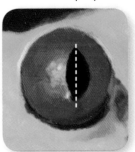

RED-EYED
TREE FROG

horizontal pupil

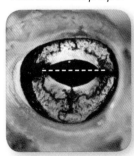

EASTERN
AMERICAN TOAD

9

The Family AMPHIBIAN

RED-EYED
TREE FROG

**Frogs and toads
are amphibians.**

All amphibians have breathable
skin and need to live in or near
water some of the time.

*A frog's skin must be super thin
to work. It sheds the old skin often to
make way for new skin. Then it eats it!
That all happens in the blink of an eye.*

CANE TOAD

Other amphibians are
caecilians and **salamanders**.

FISH CAECILIAN

FIRE SALAMANDER

Baby salamanders usually have gills until they mature and grow lungs. But although this axolotl is a salamander, it never loses its gills.

Frogs BIG and SMALL

The world's largest frog, the goliath, from Africa, can be as long as 13 inches (33 cm), and that's not counting its legs. It can weigh as much as 7 pounds (3.2 kg) — that's a lot of frog!

GOLIATH FROG

This frog is so small it fits neatly on a dime.

The world's smallest frogs are only found on the leafy floor of New Guinea's rainforest. Scientists recently discovered a kind of frog that is so tiny it is about the size of a housefly!

(Both frogs shown actual size)

A goliath frog sits in a boy's lap (far right). It is nearly as big as he is!

What Do Frogs EAT?

Frogs eat lots of different foods—
all of them alive!

Frogs eat spiders, fish, worms, and insects.

This ornate horned frog is big enough to gulp down a mouse.

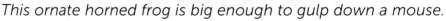

Very quickly!

A frog's tongue doesn't help it swallow. Its eyes do.
They sink down into the skull and help push food along.

How do they catch
food that flies?

This one shoots out its **long, sticky tongue!**

Frog FAMILIES

There are so many frogs and toads, and so many frog and toad families. Some lay lots of eggs, others lay just a few. Some frogs take good care of their young. Others just lay eggs and leave.

A **strawberry poison dart frog** carries a tadpole on her back. She will find a flower that holds a pool of rainwater. There she will leave the baby where it will grow into a frog.

Some frogs make foam nests by kicking water with their legs. The foam hides the eggs from predators and keeps the eggs moist.

This **marsupial frog** is so fat because she has a pouch full of eggs on her back.

Frog BABIES

Frogs change a lot as they grow up.
This special transformation is called **metamorphosis**.

A frog starts out as a little squiggle in a ball of jelly—a frog egg.

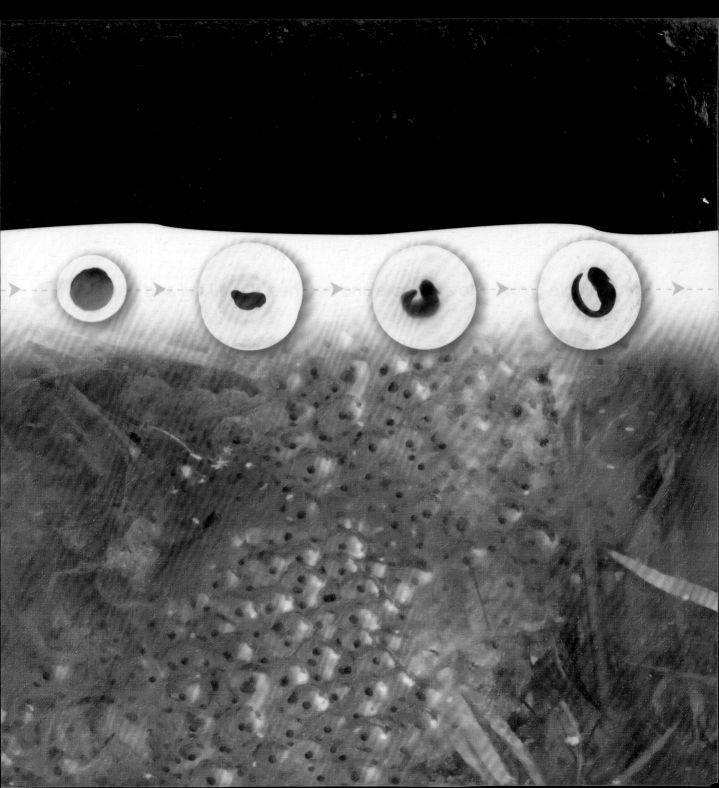

The squiggle grows into a tadpole and hatches. It is all tail and head.

The back legs
soon sprout,

and then the
front legs.

The tail disappears,
and a froglet hops
onto land.

Not every frog has a tadpole stage.
Some develop directly into froglets,
like this rain frog from Ecuador.

No other backboned animal goes
through such a complete transformation.

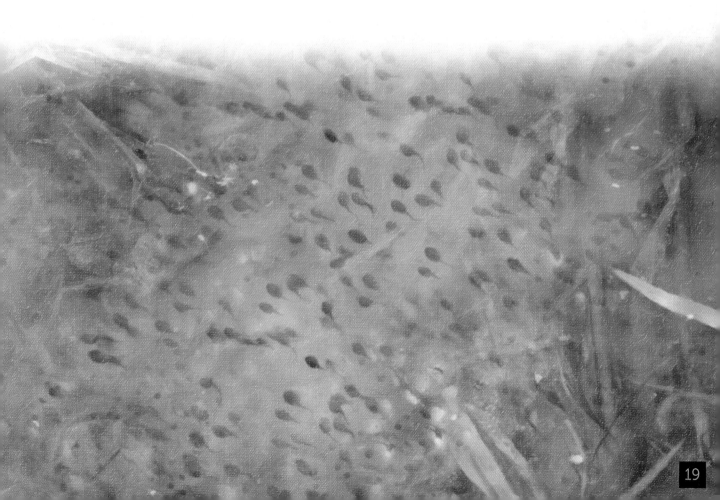

Frog SURVIVAL

Frogs are food for many animals. Some frogs hide from enemies by looking like their surroundings. This is called camouflage. Others bury themselves in the dirt or among the leaves. The tree frog below doesn't need to hide because it looks just like the other leaves.

The frog shown on the tree at left is called a mossy frog—for good reason!

This toad blends in with the surrounding mud and roots.

A tree frog or a rock? California tree frogs can change their skin color to match their surroundings.

These frogs make blending in look easy!

Can you see where the frog is, hidden by the algae?

An American toad has changed the color of his skin to blend in with the fallen leaves.

Frogs are Colorful and FASCINATING

Now that you know where to look, you can be a frog hunter. What frogs live near you?

BLUE POISON DART FROG *Poison dart frogs aren't born with poison. They get it from the food they eat.*

TOMATO FROG *It's easy to see how these tomato-red frogs got their name.*

HARLEQUIN FLYING FROG
The webbing between this frog's toes allows it to jump and glide through the air.

RED-EYED TREE FROG *This frog has sticky toes to help it climb trees.*

AFRICAN CLAWED FROG *This frog can change its appearance to match its background.*

CANE TOAD *This poisonous toad from South America was introduced in Australia, where it is now a huge pest because it has no natural predators there.*

WOOD FROG *How does this frog last through a harsh winter? By freezing solid! It thaws out in early spring.*

WAX FROG *Is it real or made from wax? These frogs stay so still!*

FIRE-BELLIED TOAD *These toads have been known to live as long as 20 years!*

Frogs in DANGER

In people, skin is what keeps out germs. Not so in frogs. Their breathable skin lets in chemicals from pollution that is making them sick. They are disappearing, which means other animals won't have food.

What can we do to take care of frogs in the future?